Essentially M
by
MARGARET E. MOONEY

Photographs by Charlie Wong

Richard C. Owen Publishers, Inc.
Katonah, New York

Me as a baby.

Writing in my favorite place.

Richard C.Owen Publishers, Inc.
PO Box 585
Katonah, New York 10536

Library of Congress Cataloging-in-Print Information

Mooney, Margaret E.
    Essentially M / by Margaret E. Mooney.
        p. cm. -- (Authors at work)
    ISBN-13: 978-1-57274-857-6
    ISBN-10: 1-57274-857-5
    1. Authorship. I. Title. II Series.

    PN147.M74 2006
    808'.02--dc22

                                                    2006040146

1. Mooney, Margaret - Juvenile literature. 2. Authors, New Zealand - 21th Century-Biography -- Juvenile literature. 3. Children's literature- Authorship - Juvenile

Literature. [1 Mooney, Margaret . 2. Authors, New Zealand] 1.Wong, Charlie, ill.
II Title . III Authors at Work (Katonah, NY)

[B]

Janice Boland   Editor, Art, and Production Director
Christine Ditmans   Editorial and Production Assistant

Printed in China

9   8   7   6   5   4   3   2   1

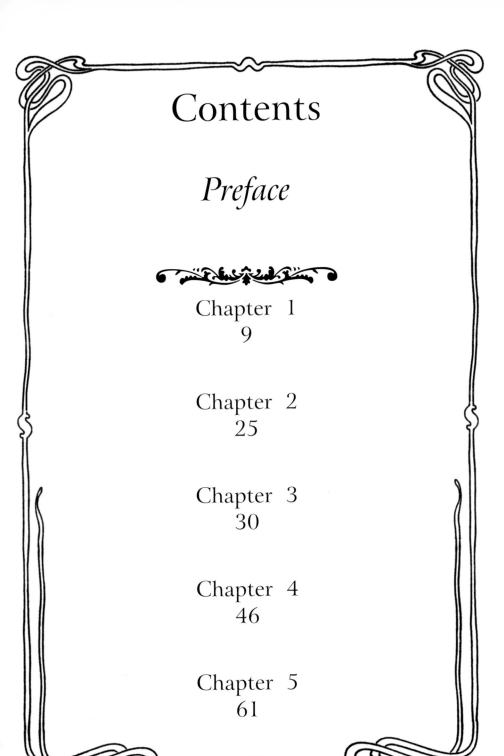

Contents

Preface

Kiwi birds.

Preface

I love writing so I was delighted when I was asked to share some of my experiences about learning to be a writer, who I am, and how important writing is in my life. However, I have been surprised at how difficult it has been to pen these words. I live in New Zealand and, although I travel a lot, I am what we call a "kiwi" (no, not the bird that cannot fly, we use that name for a person who was born in New Zealand—and especially for someone who has lived there for a long time.)

But my main audiences are American students, most of whom have not been to New Zealand. Although we may look similar (apart from my age!) and speak the same language (with an accent), we are different and see things through different eyes. However, I could only write about writing as I know it, as I learnt to write, and as I teach and practice it now.

I share some of my experiences and understandings in the first three chapters of the book. The fourth chapter is similar to an interview, as I have answered some of the questions students frequently ask about my work. There is a short concluding piece in which I tell how one group of teachers responded to my work and shared their love of books.

I hope you will find some similarities with your writing and that the differences will make you think more about what you can do with your pen, sharing your ideas and information with your audiences.

Margaret

My "Essentially M" wall quilt.

Chapter One

In my living room in front of "Essentially M."

My cousin and friend, Alison Leslie, known as Wink.

Welcome to my home. Yes! That's me beside the chair but it is also me on the wall. My cousin, Alison Leslie, made the wall quilt "Essentially M" (not the usual shape or size by any means—it's the size and shape of a body—one far more streamlined than mine), to be a "fabric biography." I know it sounds weird but it is based on my life with books. I love it!

Alison's mother and my dad were siblings. Despite living three-hundred miles apart, they were good mates in the same way that Alison and I have similar interests and understandings.

My house.

When I moved into my new house Alison made "Essentially M" as a link between the past and what we would have in common in the future. We both love anything to do with stitching and fabric. And each piece of material in this quilt recalls a chapter in my life all leading up to the open book which signifies my love for reading and writing. The book is open because Alison and I are open to new understandings. We are both life-long learners.

The bracelet signifies my love of jewelry.

My house has seven large book shelves, all crammed with books. And, because I have run out of wall space I have books in chests, drawers, and boxes. I think of reading and writing as art forms and consider the bookshelves full of wonderful artistic creations.

However, the bookshelves on one wall are art in *two* ways. People often think they are bent under the strain of the books but that is how they were designed. I wanted the shelves to be more than just storage space. Friends often joke that when the shelves appear to be straight it is a signal that it is time for them to go home.

Those shelves hold books mainly for enjoyment or for extending my vistas or views about the world. The shelves also remind me of people or events that have shaped my life.

The wood is bent to make the bookshelves appear as if floating across the wall.

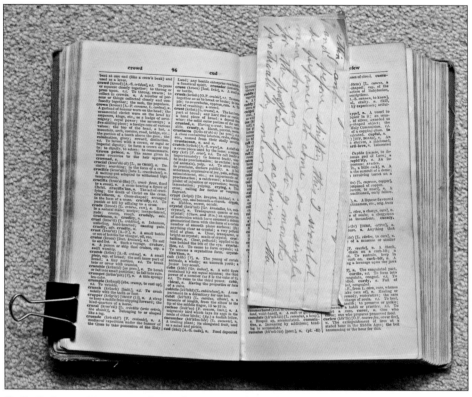

Dad's dictionary, his notes made it a dictionary within a dictionary.

At one end of the top shelf are books that belonged to my dad. Reading was important to him. He had saved money from his first job to buy classics, mainly books by Charles Dickens. His dictionary is also there.

When I was a child, Dad's dictionary was always on the end of a shelf in the kitchen. Hardly a day went by when he did not refer to it; add a scrap of paper with his own definition, or a reference to where he read the word, or how he might use it.

Those were my first lessons in a reader's and a writer's role in editing and revising.

Another bookshelf includes some of my favorite children's books. The bottom shelf holds treasures from my childhood—three "working books" (as I used to refer to them). One, from my grandmother, is a version of *Cinderella*, another is a book of stories by the famous Danish writer, Hans Christian Andersen.

My childhood books–I used to pretend that the stand-up pages were the backdrop for plays I dreamed up.

Opposite the preface of the book, "Han's Andersen's Fairy Stories"[1], a letter from "The Wizard" reads:

'These tales have stood the test of years

and still are music to young ears!

May you in time look back, as I do now

to their strange plots and cry

Though I to manhood now have grown

I still can dwell in childhood's world—

a World that's all its own.

For in that power of thinking young,

how to grow old, we learn.

These tales you'll love, these tales I prize,

and, therefore, to their urge I rise

And, with my wand's fantastic touch,

raise on these pages pictures such

As in their wonderment and grace I hope

will justify the place

And please your eye but half as well

as Hans will please your ear.'

S.L.G   The Wizard

[1] Hans Andersen's Fairy Stories. Edited and produced by S. Luis Giruad, M.R.S.L. London, Stand Publications. Date unknown.

Those books were read and reread.

Another book kept all these years has an inscription on the inside cover. It reads "Merry Christmas and Birthday Wishes From Glenys XXXXX 1952 - 53."

The Girl a much-loved present from my sister, Glenys, on my 12th birthday.

My sister was fifteen at the time, and she bought the book with her earnings from teaching piano after school and on Saturdays. It was a great sacrifice to spend such hard-earned money on a younger sister.

I loved that book!

Although I did not realize it at the time, those books and other favorites increased my competence as a reader. I was gaining fluency and expression, which were important, especially because oral reading was part of our daily reading program at school.

My many recipe books.

I also have bookshelves for books about gardening and music and for cookbooks. I have the recipe books my mother (a very good cook) used, and many of these contain her special tips or amendments to the original recipes. I keep some of my embroidery books in a chest.

Then there are books associated with my work—some are for when I am teaching, others help me with my writing, and others are about the countries where I travel to talk with teachers or visit classrooms.

Books and magazines for my work as a an author and teacher.

Before I visit a country, I try to read about some of its history and attractions. Then afterwards, I read more about its history, or I read biographies of people from the area, as well as some of the writing of the country's authors.

For example, I am very fond of Robert Frost's poems, Katherine Graham's autobiography highlighting her work as a journalist, and the biography of Alistair Cooke whose radio commentaries were heard weekly in New Zealand. These writings have helped me understand some of the cultural perspectives or aspects of life I need to remember when I am visiting the United States.

One of the bookshelves in my workroom (which I think of as my "For Now Room") I use as a dump-all. It holds the fifty or so books I have authored and some of the hundreds of books I have edited.

The bookshelf beside my computer and desk holds the journals I have kept about my learning as a teacher, writer, editor, and educational consultant. Seeing them on the shelf reminds me that learning is a continuing process.

Dotted around the house are other "special" books—current favorites, books I am now reading, a book containing scribblings of a writing project, a collection of poetry scribblings—my latest writing endeavor—and some of my handmade books. You could say my house is a mini-library.

Libraries were important during my childhood. In fact, I wanted to be a librarian and "playing libraries" was a favorite rainy day pastime. It involved placing two kitchen chairs across the doorway of my bedroom. I would open the curtain on the bookshelves to display my "books."

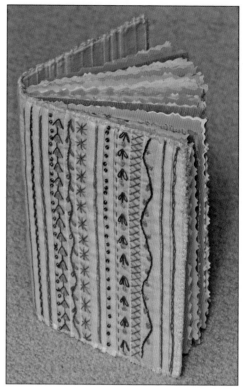

My handmade book. I embroidered the cover.

These were mainly magazines that arrived every six weeks by boat from England. As soon as a shipment arrived, I would make a library pocket and card for each one. Imaginary friends borrowed the books, their name dutifully written on the card complete with a return date. When "business" was slow I would write reviews of the magazines—so rereading and writing occupied the passing hours.

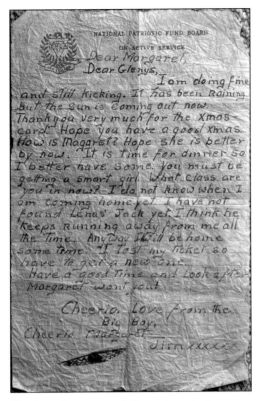

The letter from my uncle Jim written during
World War II.

My mum had nine siblings, and four of her younger brothers served in the Second World War. My treasures include a letter on tissue-thin paper written by one of her brothers while on the battlefield in Italy.

I was only a pre-schooler when Uncle Jim wrote the letter, but even then, I knew that correspondence from someone away at the war was a very important occurrence. I have several such treasures and these were a very important influence on my early writing. They taught me that writing enables us to keep in touch with those far away.

While convalescing on a hospital ship after being wounded, my uncle Fred stitched a leather horse for my grandmother. I always loved to play with the horse as a child and was delighted when it was given to me after my grandmother died. It now stands in a prominent place on my bookshelf.

Uncle Fred's horse.

I have many such treasures on my bookshelves. Actually I think of them as "treasure troves" rather than "book-shelves." My books are treasures, too, and each has many memories of how it came into my hands and of the thoughts it engendered as I read it.

My maternal grandmother.

When her brothers returned home from their war duties, Mum organized welcoming parties. These and their subsequent marriages were times of great celebration. Despite my young age, I began writing about these family gatherings and other family celebrations. My mum became very concerned that such writings should remain for "personal audience" only. In fact, I was required to make dramatic changes to some for fear someone else should read some of my views.

I learned that considering the feelings of readers is a reason for revising one's work—an early lesson in editing.

My mum in the middle row, with her brothers, Jim and Fred, top and bottom left.

A further early lesson in editing and revision occurred when I was at high school. One of our essay topics was "Money is the Root of All Evil." I sought my dad's help and vividly recall his assistance with planning, and his insistence on rewrites.

Today we would call the plan he helped me create a "graphic organizer." Writing to a plan was new to me, and it was not usual for my dad to help me to this degree. So the composition of the essay stands out in my memory, as does my teacher Mr. Robinson's comment, "A marked improvement. Worthy of an A. Keep it up!"

The corner with some of my dad's books. The china dog was also his.

But over and above this is the memory that my dad insisted on more rewrites than I had ever done before. The "A" from Mr. Robinson was important, but not as important or satisfying as my dad's endorsement and my learning about the importance of rewriting. I had learned what it meant to achieve "standard."

My favorite photo of my dad.

Another early lesson in the rewards of revision and rewriting was one I experienced vicariously through my sister. We both took piano lessons. She went on to become a very accomplished pianist. While she obviously had musical talent and aptitude, her high level of achievement came as a result of the way she practiced.

My sister Glenys.

She would play the same piece over and over until it met her standard and what she knew our piano teacher would expect. I, on the other hand, either fudged practice or would dash through a piece, seldom correcting mistakes. Those mistakes became habits and my piano playing became a battle between me and my teacher.

Revision and editing is part of a self-improving system in whatever we pursue. I could revise and edit my writing—why couldn't I do the same with my piano playing is a question I have pondered many times since.

As I write this, I am thinking about the "editing" I do as I embroider or quilt. Some days I do more unstitching than stitching. Sometimes I take out every stitch and start all over again. I had never thought of my "unstitching" as editing—but that is exactly what it is. I am thinking about making the piece the best it can be for its intended purpose and how I want to be able to view it in the future.

Chapter Two

At a workshop in Fiji.

I started my teaching career teaching my favorite subjects—reading and writing. I loved my work but I now think of those years as preparation for my second career—editing and writing.

I began my editing career as editor for New Zealand's national reading program for the first three years of school. This proved to be a major stepping stone to many challenging opportunities and new experiences. It opened the door to my career as an editor and a writer while still enabling me to keep in touch with teachers and students in classrooms.

Books I edited, still in use in New Zealand schools.

Authors had been invited to submit manuscripts and submit they did—not tens or even hundreds. By the end of the first year I had edited over a thousand manuscripts using the five criteria, which I still use.

1. Does the piece have "charm, magic, impact and appeal?" I think of this as what will remain in the reader's head. What chunks of language or meaning will come flooding back long after the book has been closed?

2. Is the idea worthwhile? Does the piece give sufficient payback for the time and effort the reader will spend reading?

3. Does the structure suit the piece? How does the author cause the reader to stick with the piece? Is there an identifiable beginning, middle, and ending?

4. Is the language appropriate? Does the vocabulary and the way the piece is crafted reflect the author's consideration of the topic, the purpose, and the probable audience?

5. Does the piece avoid stereotyping? Are the character's credible? Do their actions and words reflect who they are? Will the piece offend anyone?

Over the years I have added additional questions. But these five are at the heart of planning, drafting, revising, editing, and deciding whether or not a piece is ready for a wider audience.

Not long after beginning my editorial work, I attended a seminar where thirty top New Zealand children's book authors each brought a new piece of their work to be shared and critiqued by the group.

Watching the angst or anxiety as each one read their piece, (as my supervisor said, "bared their souls through their pens") and waited for their colleagues to discuss it, was a lesson for me in the personal nature of writing.

Reading your work to a group is not easy. You are reading your words, but at the same time you are listening to them through the ears of everyone in the group. Each manuscript stands naked and defenseless. Comments from a group seem to make the minute into huge issues.

Lesson number one: the audience for the first oral reading should be yourself as writer, reader, and listener.

Lesson number two came hard on the heels of that writer's seminar. I had to present the first set of manuscripts I had selected and edited to a committee.

I went into the meeting feeling positive about the manuscripts and my ability to defend them against any criticism or questions. I knew those manuscripts like the back of my hand.

But hearing someone else read them made me see them through another pair of eyes and ears. The expression and pace of another reader changed the emphasis and, in some cases, the meaning. It is hard to be objective about anything you have worked on. Though hard to achieve, objectivity is necessary.

Lesson number three: we read what we think is on the paper. I was awakened about three o'clock one morning by my printer asking if we really wanted a sentence that did not make sense. The word "the" had been omitted from one of the pages of a book we were publishing. Several people had read that manuscript and we had all read what we thought was there.

Pointing to each word while reading is not the prerogative of beginning readers—experienced writers also need to resort to it when editing!

Chapter Three

My editing lessons continued—and still continue. The more I learn about writing, the more I want to write. The more I understand about *how* I write, the more I know how I need to revise and edit my work.

Weeding in the garden as I rehearse my manuscripts.

For example, I spend a long time planning what I will write. I rehearse the first section in my head, perhaps while gardening or driving somewhere. When I sit down to write, I go at full speed making careless errors and not attending to detail.

Once I get underway, I need to go back to the beginning and slowly and carefully check my work. This gives me another burst of thinking ahead, another planning boost, and off I go again. I might only write two or three sentences before rereading it to make sure that the text is as I want it to be and so my audience will see my view clearly.

I know I would find revision and editing a burden if I left it all until the end; and my writing pace would decrease. Each burst of revision gives me fresh impetus to "get going" again.

I often put my first draft on to my laptop and take it outside to tap away in the garden.

Writing in bursts means I need to be very careful about transitions. It is easy to start a new thought as if it were a new piece of writing; so I have to make sure there is a flow from one section to another. Good transitions require more than a linking word or two. Most need to be embedded in both the section that has preceeded, as well as what follows.

I expect my readers to bring some background knowledge and to be able to view my information and ideas from my perspective. That means that when I reread my work I need to ask what I have left for my reader to bring. Have I assumed too much?

I abhor books that condescend to their reader but I also find it frustrating when an author leaves me with too much work to do to get inside his or her head. Striking a good balance is hard.

I find I need to let a piece of writing "sit" for a few days and then take a fresh look at it. Sometimes, that is not possible because I have left the writing until the deadline is upon me. I know then, that there will be a lot of red pen marks from the editor!

When I was teaching, I often asked my students to hand their work in on a set day. I would keep it for a few days, and then hand it back and ask them to reread it before we would "mark" it together. It was always interesting to watch as they reread their words. Their editing pens would be working overtime.

Talking with students about their writing.

My preference is writing informational text or texts based on my own experiences. I have recently started writing poetry and this has made me aware of some aspects of my writing that had completely escaped my notice.

At my laptop.

I have always known that I work best in the early hours of the morning. But, until I started trying to write poetry I did not think very much about *where* I write.

I find it easier to write in poetic form when I am in unfamiliar surroundings or when I am seeing something for the first time, or seeing it in a new way.

I am not sure why this is so. Perhaps it is because I am very conscious of selecting just the right words to "label" the new experience or insight in order to remember it.

Perhaps that is the reason why I always seem to end up taking the thought back into myself. I am probably thinking "Why do I need to remember this?" Learning more about oneself is one of the great benefits of writing.

I find that I need to record where I was at the time and what prompted me to pick up my pen. I believe that is another aspect of thinking about the importance of the thought or experience.

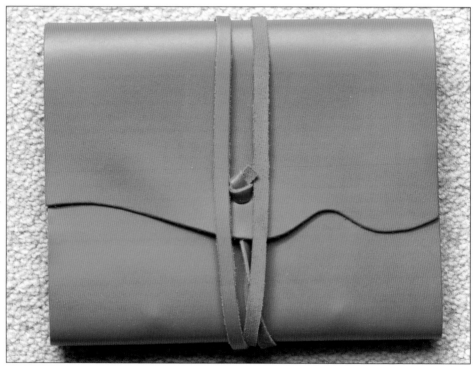

My locked book of poems.

I consider my poetry to be "for my eyes only." I even keep my efforts locked in a leather bound book. However, I will share *Erik's Place* with you as an example of these understandings about my work.

I visit the United States three or four times each year, and always try to spend time with my friends in Seattle. On this particular visit they were eager to show me the landscaping work they had done in the ravine on their property.

The ferny path to Erik's Place.

Erik, their two year-old grandson was also visiting. His first thought was to get down to the "wawa" to be Christopher Robin throwing sticks into the water and running to the other side of the bridge to watch them float downstream.

Erik's Place

They cleared the vines, created paths

Built a bridge and stacked stone walls

To take us from humdrum of life

To Nature's harmony.

A place for thought for those of age

And Pooh sticks for the young.

A seat for Erik at wawa's edge

Beneath the leafy green

A world apart yet all within

The gifts that Nature brings–

The world that only thought can bring

For Nature to enhance.

One tiny boy at peace with self

No greater woes than which stick next

To ripple up the stream

Where are the gentle streams we once enjoyed

The calm is there no more

What paths and bridges did man ignore

What hearts stacked walls of stone

How did our lives become entangled vines

And peace flee out the door?

It's time to play Pooh sticks again

And watch the waters flow

To enjoy the joy young ones can bring

To follow in their world

To make the rushing waters smooth

To see our face therein.

One chance is all we get these days

It's time to mend our ways.

MEM 2/7/04

As I retyped the poem, I changed some of the punctuation. I find it difficult to let a piece go—there is always something to change, add, or delete. Perhaps a piece is *never* finished.

I read some of my work that has been published and, even after the most skillful editing, it seems as if there is still something not quite as it could be. I guess this is because we bring new levels of understanding to each subsequent reading. Also our emotions and the attention we devote to the reading influence how we perceive a piece. Writing is an ever-changing process.

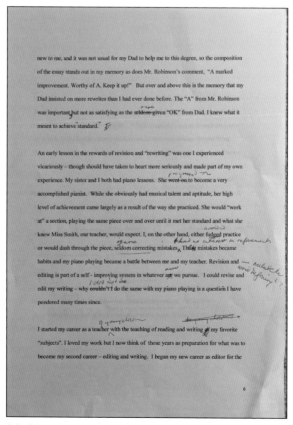

I find it easier to edit on hard copy.

Off again to new places and learning.

My mum holding her first grandchild.

My work as an editor took me to countries I longed to visit but never dreamed I would. I went to Vanuatu, the Philippines, Fiji, Samoa, England, Sweden, Canada, and of course, to the United States. My mum would follow my trips abroad with great interest. So I kept a detailed diary of the places I visited and people I met. Not only did she read every word I wrote, but she would lend my journals to her friends.

After Mum died, my prime audience was no longer there and her friends were no longer sharing my visits through Mum's eyes. The chain of readers had been broken and there seemed no reason to keep a travel diary. It was at that stage that I started trying to write in different forms, especially poetry. Even if time does not heal, it does bring new opportunities.

Painting of Niagra Falls by Frederick Edwin Church.

One of the exciting aspects about writing is that each piece is different and has its own peculiarities. Picking up the pen begins a domino effect. This was especially noticeable with the "before" and "after" of writing *A Matter of Balance*.

In this book I write about some of The Great Blondin's escapades crossing Niagara Falls. The Great Blondin was a Frenchman named Jean François Gravelet, who in 1859 made history by being the first person to cross Niagara Falls on a tightrope.

My visit to the Falls had me spellbound as I watched people in the *Maid of the Mist* boat disappear behind the huge sheet of water and then reappear seemingly unperturbed. I wandered up to the bookstore and was delighted to see children reading and chattering about some of the books.

My *teacher ears* had me eavesdropping as they chatted about "this crazy guy who did such neat stuff on a tightrope." The word "stuff" sent bells ringing so I picked up one of the books and was fascinated, but also disbelieving of what I read. I checked other books and found similar facts.

As soon as I arrived back home in New Zealand I did further research before I wrote the manuscript for *A Matter of Balance*. That was an exciting project and proved to be a starting point.

The cover of my book.

The book brought a flood of mail from readers wanting to know more details, asking how I was sure of my facts, and one or two querying the number of minutes it had taken Blondin on each of his crossings to traverse the Falls.

An early engraving of Niagra Falls.

Apart from being a reminder that getting facts right in an informational book is crucial, the correspondence reaffirmed that readers think critically about what they read.

The letters continue to arrive. Such correspondence is a pleasing reward of one's writing efforts.

The only copy of my treasured alphabet book.

One of my treasures is an alphabet book made for me by the editors and art directors when I left my editorial job. The book entitled *The Unexpurgated* is a wonderful reminder of my years as an editor. It is almost twenty years since I received the book, but I look at it frequently and never fail to be inspired to pick up a pen and write.

Sometimes I just jot down memories of some of those colleagues who contributed to the book. Sometimes I write a note to one of them. Sometimes my writing bears no resemblance to anything of that period of my life, but I just feel inspired to write.

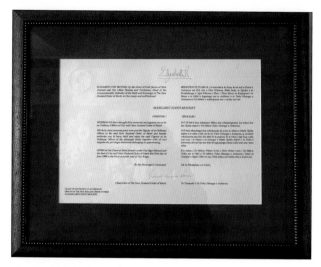

Queen Elizabeth's signature is at the top of the certificate.

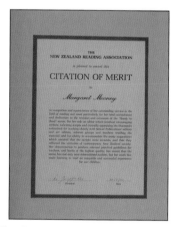

The Citation of Merit "for outstanding work in the field of reading".

The Zealand Order of Merit is worn on official occasions.

On the wall of my workroom is the Citation of Merit I received from the New Zealand Reading Association for my work in teaching reading and my work in developing and editing children's books. Alongside it is an award from Queen Elizabeth II of England, a one-in-a-million honor. Both awards were surprises. Though these awards are in my name, they also belong to the community of writers who have nurtured my reading and writing in a myriad of ways.

People often say that writing is a lonely occupation. In some ways it can be when you are digging into your head for ideas or tapping away on the computer during the pre-dawn hours. But in other ways it is a social activity because most writing depends on one's interactions with the outside world.

We are spurred into writing by what we see, feel, or think about as we go about our daily lives. Other people or things present the opportunity to write—or paint or compose music—the challenge is to take the opportunity and find joy in doing so.

Chapter Four

Writing is an individual activity. Each author's voice, style, and pattern of working differ. While authors are often asked the same questions, the answers vary. I have summarized my responses to some of those frequently-asked questions in the hope that they may help my readers understand the challenges and joys of writing.

Q: *Do you write your drafts on the computer?*

A: *I rarely use the computer until I have a piece underway. Before I actually start writing I spend a lot of time thinking and rehearsing in my head. Then when I finally think I am ready to put pen to paper, I sharpen several pencils, clean an eraser, gather paper or select the exercise book I plan to use, and set myself at my desk or at the dining table or in my favorite chair.*

The ceramic seat outside my bedroom, a good place for planning and recording the first thoughts of the day.

If the weather is suitable, I will often take my work outside. I turn on the fountains and sit on the ceramic seat outside my bedroom. The fountains are small and surrounded by a birdbath, so I am often distracted by the birds as they splatter and splash or perch on the edge of the birdbath preening themselves. I sat out there this morning to draft some of this manuscript and was delighted to hear the tui's beautiful song as he sat in the kowhai tree nearby. Although easily distracted, I can refocus much more easily when outside than when I am inside where there is always other work to be done.

Once I get a piece of writing underway I can work on the computer but I have to print it when I want to revise or edit. I go through a lot of paper printing a few pages, working on them, and then printing them again along with the next new section.

Early morning at the computer.

Q: *How do you distinguish revising from editing?*

A: *I see revising as honing and shaping a draft so the manuscript says what I want it to say. Editing is when I think more about the ease with which my work can be read. Editing has more to do with accuracy.*

But I do not think of them as totally separate. When I am revising a piece, transposing a section, or expanding or deleting, my eye is also picking up some of the spelling or punctuation errors or attending to grammar or layout.

However, when I do a final read and my attention is on editorial elements of accuracy and conventions, I will also make necessary changes to the shape or sequence or replace a word or phrase.

Revision is when I am thinking about the craft of writing.

Editing is when I am focusing on the mechanics.

Both are essential. It is no good having the most creative ideas in the world if others cannot access or understand them. And it is useless being meticulous about spelling, grammar, and conventions if you have nothing worthwhile to say.

Revising and editing before someone else reads your work are ways of safeguarding or protecting your ideas, helping to keep them and your voice intact.

Q: *How do you plan or organize your writing?*

A: *I often organize in my head. I sometimes use graphic organizers to sort my thoughts and to keep track of where I am in achieving my intention. And I often use a graphic organizer when I am gathering information, or taking notes. I find them helpful in noting key words and in keeping me on task. But most of all I use them to remind me of the kind of thinking I need to keep in focus.*

For example, if the piece is to compare one set of experiences or features with another, I might use a T chart. If the writing is to show a sequence, a T chart would not work, so I might use an organizer.

Once I have written my ideas down, I then use the organizer or my notes as a check when writing. I actually put a check mark as I include an idea. I revise the plan as I write so my organizer becomes very messy—but it is a working document. I use it as a measure of my progress, and then as a check at the end when rereading my complete piece.

Q: *Which part of the writing process do you find the most challenging?*

A: *That depends on the piece, how comfortable I feel with what I know, and why I am writing it. In my own reading, I find it difficult to commit to a book if there is too much scene setting or explanations of relationships between characters. So I am very conscious of beginnings and often struggle with getting started, but once I am underway I am able to work into the piece and enjoy the work.*

When I was teaching I would often say to the students, "Let's start reading this book at this page rather than the beginning. This is where the action really begins."

Sometimes I find every part of writing hard. Sometimes ideas just don't flow. I have learned that rather than struggle for too long and get frustrated with myself, I am better off diverting my attention for a little while and then going back to it. I know that this is not possible to do in the classroom and that, when writing at home, it is too easy to stay diverted. I have taught myself some techniques that seem to work for me.

Sometimes I think about something that I have written that causes me to smile or feel proud of my efforts. (I guess I am convincing myself that I am a writer.)

Sometimes I wonder how another author would approach the task; or I go to one of my bookshelves, browse for a few minutes, and then try to settle down.

My journals, a record of my learning, hold many stories.

Sometimes I struggle with the ending. I want the reader to feel satisfied, even if they do not agree with what I have said. Some writers say they often have the ending before they start writing. That has never happened to me—maybe it would make life easier.

Then there are days when my mind seems crowded with other thoughts and the pen just won't flow. On those occasions I walk around the garden, have a cup of coffee, or just hope that I will be able to work at double-pace the next day.

My task board helps me focus and meet deadlines.

Q: *Do you write every day?*

A: *Yes, I keep a list of current projects beside my computer. Each morning at 5 a.m. I check my e-mail. New Zealand time is different than Eastern U.S.A. time and if someone wants a response I need to attend to it early in my day. Then, I look at my list and see what needs immediate attention. It may well be a letter or something I need to prepare for the work I am doing in a school. I try to work on a manuscript every day when I am home.*

When I travel (which is frequently) I find it difficult to work on manuscripts, so I have to try to be very organized and focused about writing when I'm home.

People often think that authors write on a whim—far from it. Good authors are very organized about their work—and that is something I am working on improving. I have spent time re-organizing my files and have promised myself that I will keep my desk tidy. Unfortunately, it is not the first time I have made this promise!

A few of my published books.

Q: *You have written books for young readers and books for teachers. Which do you prefer? Is one easier than the other?*

A: *They each have their challenges. When writing for young readers, I am reminded of George Bernard Shaw's words that you have to "write with a sharp pen."*

You cannot use too many words and every word you do use has to matter. I have a pile of manuscripts for possible children's book that may never go beyond my filing cabinet. From time to time I take them out, read them, lose courage to send them off, and just file them again. I call it my "round again file." A friend once asked me if I kept re-filing them because I was afraid of them being rejected by a publisher. The answer is a definite "No." I just know that only the best will do for beginning readers and that means a special skill is required. I want to continue writing for children although it's so much harder than writing for adults.

Q: *How do you feel when one of your pieces gets published?*

A: *It depends how much input I have had during the publishing process. I do have some books that I have not opened because I did not see the edited version before they were illustrated or went to print. I feel as if the idea has been stolen from me and that hurt. It has had a profound effect on how I edit students' writing.*

This student made changes to his manuscript before reading it to me.

Student's edited writing.

I believe that I need to be with my students as they write, in the same way as I am with them when they read a book. I should not wait until they finish a piece of writing before I offer guidance or respond to their questions.

I don't mark their papers with a red pen, but use the same color pen for editing as they use for writing. Then my marks do not dominate and the student has to read carefully instead of hopping from one mark to another, correcting without much thought.

Q: *Does writing pay well, is it lucrative?*

A: *Not for me! Definitely not! If I relied solely on writing for an income, I would be in deep poverty.*

My fountain, birdbath, and seat bought with royalties.

Royalty checks from publishers arrive every six months. When I receive my checks, I combine the amounts and buy something special that will remind me to be grateful to those who bought my work. I have several ceramic pieces in my yard that have been bought with royalties—the birdbath and fountains, two ceramic seats, and a bird house.

Q: *You have been an editor so why do you still need an editor for your work?*

A: *It is very difficult to be objective about your own work. An author writes as he/she wants others to see the ideas or information. An editor acts on behalf of both the author and the reader so asks different questions of the writing. The author says, "This is how it is." The editor asks, "What is this really saying? Is that what the author wants it to say and will readers see it the same way?" An editor's task is to safeguard the integrity of the ideas or information, and that can be a real challenge with some manuscripts.*

Q: *How do you keep learning about writing?*

A: *There's an oft-quoted saying that the more you read, the more you can read, and the more you want to read. I think that also applies to writing. My writing improves each time I really apply myself to a writing task.*

I also talk with friends who are writers. Some will read my manuscripts. Some friends will allow me to test or trial my work with students or teachers. I know I will often need to make changes, for I always learn something about my writing as a result of trialing.

And I read a lot.

I have several favorite authors whose work I reread many times. One of my favorites is Owen Marshall, a New Zealand short story writer who has a wonderful turn of phrase and who can make the most ordinary every day occurrence very interesting. His descriptions of characters leave me smiling and thinking about people I know who have similar characteristics. I have learned a lot about good beginnings from reading and thinking about Owen Marshall's work.

I really enjoy reading Margaret Mahy's books. She is another New Zealand author, in fact, she is considered by many people to be the best author of children's fiction.

I had the honor of working with Margaret Mahy when I was doing editorial work and her humility, sharp brain, vivid imagination, and amazing vocabulary broadened my horizons about books and writing. I have just finished reading "A Writer's Life" an excellent biography of Margaret Mahy by Tessa Duder, another New Zealand writer. Tessa and Margaret Mahy knew each other and both are authors, so Tessa knew her subject very well. It made me think about the times I have tried to write about a topic before I knew enough about it.

Every two years I attend a Writer's Festival in Wellington (New Zealand's capital city) where authors and poets of international acclaim read and discuss some of their work. It is a really exciting and motivating time. Sessions might be presented by a poet from Israel, a journalist from Canada, a children's author from Britain, and a novelist from Pakistan.

I attend the festival with two friends and we spend many hours discussing the day's events. As each author's work is available for sale we always come home laden with books.

The author Margaret Mahy.

With my two friends, Anne and Edith.

Another way that I learn about writing is by going back and reading some of my earlier work and setting myself new goals to work towards. I did this recently and discovered to my horror that I had too many long and rambling sentences. (I have been mindful of that as I have been rereading this manuscript.)

The more I know about writing, the more there is to know. That is what makes it such an exciting adventure.

Chapter Five

Sitting in my favorite spot.

I started this book by writing about "Essentially M," the quilt made by my cousin, Alison. I want to end it by telling you about another quilt.

One day last week, the courier van sped up the driveway and a large carton was delivered to my door. I saw it was from the United States. I recognized the sender's name, Margaret Redinger, a teacher at Farwell Elementary School on the outskirts of Spokane, Washington.

"What on earth could Margaret be sending me?" I asked as I undid the tape.

These students loved finding their favorite books on my Farwell quilt.

Out tumbled the biggest quilt I have ever seen. I have visited the school several times and always enjoy working with the teachers as we try to understand more about teaching reading and writing. Our discussions include thinking about and sharing books.

Margaret had put together a book quilt!

Each of the teachers and assistants at the school had chosen a book. Margaret made a fifteen-inch cloth square for each book, which the teachers signed. Then she sewed the squares into a double-sided quilt. She must have known that I was buying a new and bigger bed.

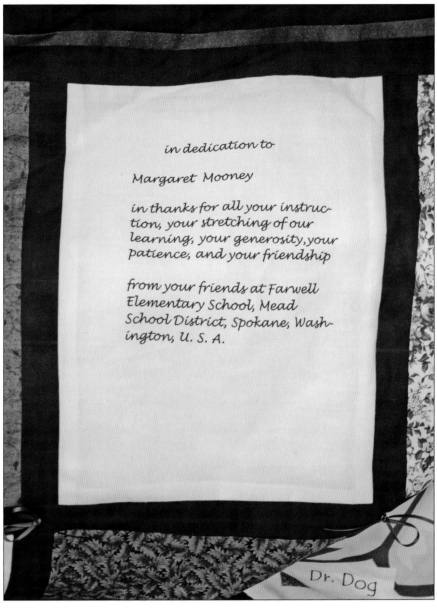

in dedication to

Margaret Mooney

in thanks for all your instruction, your stretching of our learning, your generosity, your patience, and your friendship

from your friends at Farwell Elementary School, Mead School District, Spokane, Washington, U. S. A.

Dr. Dog

My Farwell Quilt dedication.

Now not only will I read and write books by day as I sit in the chair by my "Essentially M Quilt", I will also sleep under the cloth books in my "Farwell Quilt."

And close by, I will have pen and paper ready to record ideas, dream-
ings, and yearnings, remind myself of tasks to be done, write a note to
a friend, jot down a phrase or snippet, make a revision to a manuscript
or—just simply let my thoughts flow.